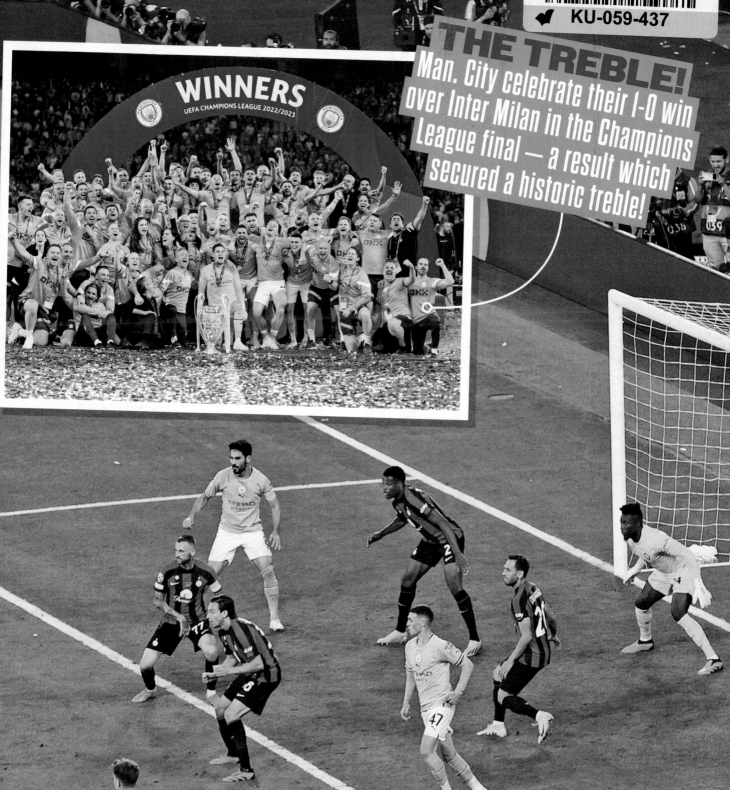

WINNERS
UEFA CHAMPIONS LEAGUE 2022/2023

THE TREBLE!
Man. City celebrate their 1-0 win over Inter Milan in the Champions League final — a result which secured a historic treble!

WELCOME!

WOW! IT'S FAIR TO SAY 2023 has been an incredible year of football — full of drama, excitement and incredible achievements. Join us as we take a look back at the biggest moments and celebrate the heroes of the game! Happy reading! *GARY*

WHAT'S IN YOUR MOTD MAG ANNUAL?

P10 JUDE BELLINGHAM!

P40 TOP 10 GOALS!

P62 EURO 2024!

THE BIG WINNERS OF 2023!

MAN. CITY
PREMIER LEAGUE CHAMPIONS

City won their fifth Prem title in six years, despite trailing Arsenal by five points with just two months to go!

MAN. CITY
FA CUP WINNERS

Two weeks after winning the Prem. Pep Guardiola led his team to the double. They beat Man. United 2-1 in the final!

MAN. CITY
CHAMPIONS LEAGUE WINNERS

City made it a historic treble in Istanbul when they beat Inter Milan 1-0 to win the Champions League for the first time!

ERLING HAALAND
PREMIER LEAGUE GOLDEN BOOT

Haaland smashed the Prem's goal record in his first season at the Etihad — he scored 36 goals in just 35 games!

MAN. UNITED
EFL CUP WINNERS

Erik ten Hag got his hands on some silverware in his first season at Old Trafford when his side beat Newcastle 2-0!

96 PAGES OF FOOTY FUN!

WHO'S YOUR G.O.A.T.?

LEGENDS • ICONS • RIVALS

LIONEL MESSI OR CRISTIANO RONALDO

It's time to decide once and for all who really is the greatest of all time!

P70 MESSI v RONALDO!

THE BEST OF THE BEST!

We reveal the top 30 players in women's football — does YOUR hero make our list?

P86 TOP 30 WOMEN BALLERS!

SUPERSTAR DREAM TEAM POSTERS!

Who's made our all-star line-up for 2023? Check out the posters in this annual to find out!

Rule 1: only ONE player per nation!
Rule 2: There is no rule 2!

THE LOL! ZONE!

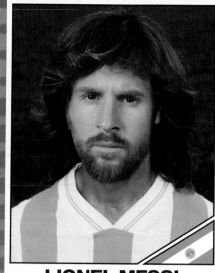

LIONEL MESSI
ARGENTINA FORWARD

FOOTY STAR REWIND!

We've imagined what today's superstars would have looked like if they'd played 30 years ago!

THOMAS MULLER
GERMANY FORWARD

VIRGIL VAN DIJK
NETHERLANDS CENTRE-BACK

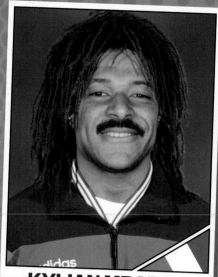

KYLIAN MBAPPE
FRANCE FORWARD

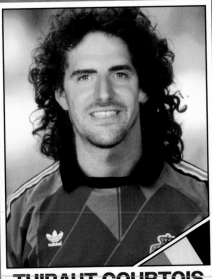

THIBAUT COURTOIS
BELGIUM KEEPER

NEYMAR
BRAZIL FORWARD

ROY'S ANIMAL IMPRESSIONS!

Crystal Palace boss Roy Hodgson is a man of many faces!

HEY ROY... DO YOUR LONG-EARED OWL!

HEY ROY... DO YOUR BABY MACAQUE!

HEY ROY... DO YOUR FRENCH MASTIFF!

HEY ROY... DO YOUR RED PANDA!

HEY ROY... DO YOUR HEDGEHOG!

HEY ROY... DO YOUR SQUIRREL!

HEY ROY... DO YOUR MEERKAT!

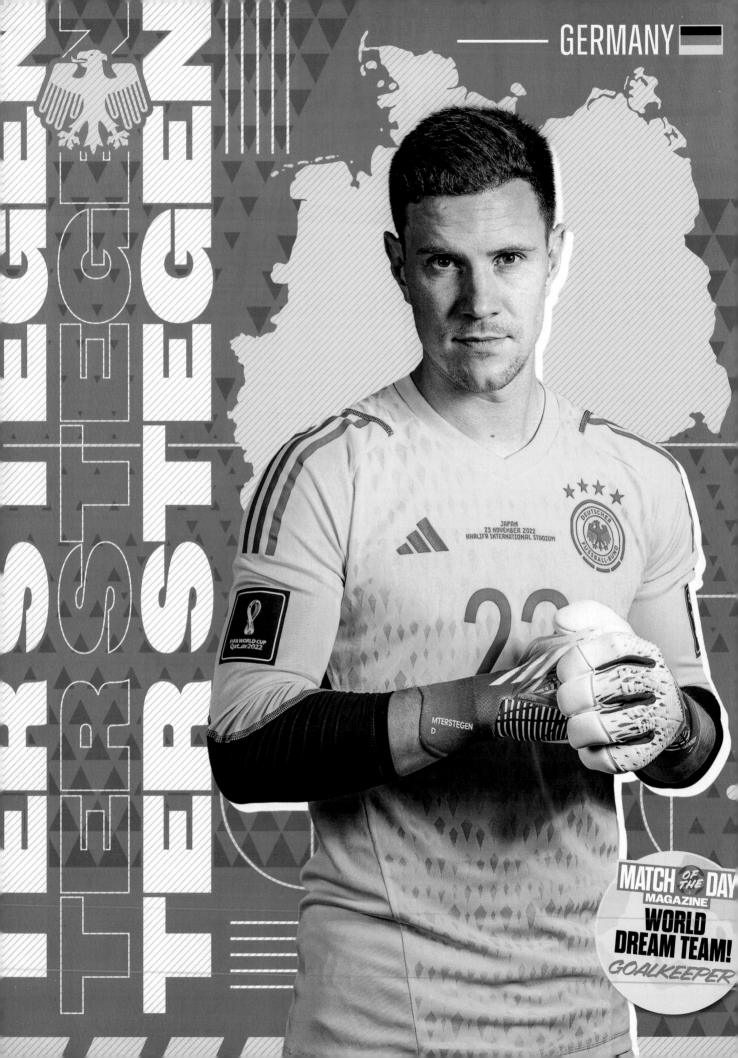

THE CHAMPIONS QUIZ!

Ooh, shiny!

These clubs have won the **MOST LEAGUE TITLES** in their country – but where do they come from?

1 COLO COLO

- **A** Uruguay
- **B** Chile
- **C** Ecuador

2 GALATASARAY

1905

- **A** Bulgaria
- **B** Turkey
- **C** Greece

3 RIVER PLATE

- **A** Mexico
- **B** Brazil
- **C** Argentina

4 AJAX

- **A** Netherlands
- **B** Belgium
- **C** Denmark

5 ANDERLECHT

- **A** Romania
- **B** Belgium
- **C** Switzerland

6 LINFIELD

- **A** Wales
- **B** Northern Ireland
- **C** Republic of Ireland

7 BENFICA

- **A** Spain
- **B** Portugal
- **C** Serbia

8 JUVENTUS

- **A** France
- **B** Germany
- **C** Italy

9 LA GALAXY

- **A** Australia
- **B** USA
- **C** India

YOUR FOOTY BRAIN POWER

YOUR SCORE ☐ /9

9	GENIUS
7	PROFESSIONAL
5	SEMI-PRO
3	AMATEUR
1	SUNDAY LEAGUE
0	OH NO, DISASTER

ANSWERS ON PAGE 92!

HEY JUDE BELLINGHAM

JUDE'S JOURNEY FROM BIRMINGHAM TO THE BERNABEU!

This is the story of a little boy from the Midlands set to become a megastar in Madrid!

THE RECORD BREAKING ROAD TO REAL!

1 THE STORY BEGINS IN STOURBRIDGE IN 2003...

Jude Victor William Bellingham is born on 29 June 2003, in Stourbridge, in the West Midlands. His dad Mark, a police sergeant, was a prolific goalscorer in non-League football — netting more than 700 goals in his playing days!

FROM UNDER-8s TO THE CHAMPIONSHIP...

Little seven-year-old Jude joins the Under-8s of his local pro club Birmingham and works his way up through the youth teams at St. Andrew's. Just after turning 16, the talented teenager is handed the No.22 shirt for the 2019-20 Championship season — this is his big chance!

2

ST. ANDREW'S STAR IS BORN...

3

It doesn't take long for Jude to take that chance. He becomes Birmingham's youngest-ever player when he makes his debut in August 2019, aged only 16. A few weeks later, he also becomes their youngest-ever scorer when he nets a winner against Stoke!

4

Despite playing just 44 games for the club, Birmingham retire the No.22 shirt in Jude's honour!

TIME TO SAY BYE BYE, BLUES...

By the end of the season, he is in demand — Man. United and Borussia Dortmund are battling it out for his signature. Enticed by Dortmund's record of developing young players, he joins them for £25 million in July 2020 — making him the most expensive 17-year-old in history!

DREAM DEBUT...

Jude makes his debut for his new club in the first match of the 2020-21 season — a German Cup match. He stars and scores in a thumping 5-0 win, and it means that, aged just 17, he had become Dortmund's youngest-ever goalscorer!

5

Dortmund, inspired by Bellingham, go on to win the cup that season — it's Jude's first trophy!

6

THE RECORDS CONTINUE TO TUMBLE...

The following month, when Dortmund face Lazio in the Champions League group stage, Bellingham becomes the youngest Englishman to start a UCL match, breaking the record previously set by Phil Foden!

JUDE IS THE REAL DEAL...

7

After three seasons in Germany, in which he wins the German Cup, the Bundesliga Player of the Year, and the hearts of the German fans, he decides to leave Dortmund. In June 2023, he joins Real Madrid for £88.5m — a fee which could eventually rise to £115m. He's made the big time!

JUDE'S PHOTO SCRAPBOOK...

NOVEMBER 2020
He makes his England debut against the Republic of Ireland at Wembley, becoming England's third-youngest player of all time!

JULY 2020
Following his record-breaking move to Borussia Dortmund, a huge mural appears in his home city of Birmingham!

APRIL 2021
Jude celebrates his first Champions League goal in a huge quarter-final clash against Man. City — a strike which sees him become Dortmund and England's youngest UCL scorer!

JUNE 2021
Despite having played just 29 top-flight games, 17-year-old Jude is called up to the England squad for Euro 2020!

JUNE 2021
Jude comes on in England's opening Euro 2020 match, a 1-0 win over Croatia, and becomes the youngest player in the history of the Euros!

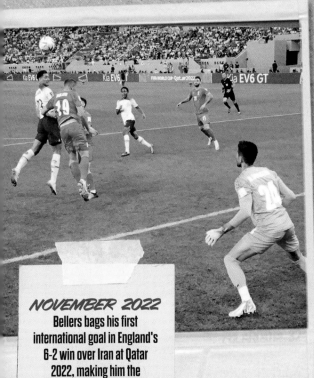

DECEMBER 2022
Jude celebrates England's last-16 World Cup win over Senegal in the Al Bayt Stadium. His Three Lions team-mate Phil Foden says: "I think he will be the best midfielder in the world!"

NOVEMBER 2022
Bellers bags his first international goal in England's 6-2 win over Iran at Qatar 2022, making him the second-youngest scorer for England at a World Cup!

MAY 2023
Bellingham laps up the applause after scoring in Borussia Dortmund's 5-2 over Borussia Monchengladbach — it turns out to be his last game for the club!

JUNE 2023
Jude bags his big move to Real Madrid and also bags the No.5 shirt, the number of his childhood idol Zinedine Zidane, who was a legend at the Bernabeu!

HOW TALL

FEET

Take a look to see how you measure up against the world's best ballers — as well as the stars of the animal kingdom!

Get an adult or a mate to measure how tall you are!

MY HEIGHT	
FT	INS

11
10
9
8
7
6
5
4
3
2
1
0

KANGAROO
5ft 10in

MOHAMED SALAH
5ft 9in

LIONEL MESSI
5ft 7in

ORANGUTAN
4ft 5in

BISON
5ft 8in

GENTOO PENGUIN
2ft 6in

16

ARE YOU?

FEET

GRIZZLY BEAR
9ft 6in

POLAR BEAR
10ft 0in

OSTRICH
9ft 0in

MARCUS
RASHFORD
5ft 11in

ERLING
HAALAND
6ft 4in

SON
HEUNG-MIN
6ft 0in

THIBAUT
COURTOIS
6ft 6in

11
10
9
8
7
6
5
4
3
2
1
0

17

DI LORENZO

GIOVANNI

ITALY

THE 5-A-SIDE WORLD CUP!

We've picked the ultimate 5-a-side team from each continent — but how do you rate them?

AFRICA

Andre **Onana**
CAMEROON

Achraf **Hakimi**
MOROCCO

Ismael **Bennacer**
ALGERIA

Mohamed **Salah**
EGYPT

Victor **Osimhen**
NIGERIA

Mohamed Salah

ASIA

Mathew **Ryan**
AUSTRALIA

Kim **Min-jae**
SOUTH KOREA

Daichi **Kamada**
JAPAN

Son **Heung-Min**
SOUTH KOREA

Kaoru **Mitoma**
JAPAN

Son Heung-Min

EUROPE

Thibaut **Courtois**
BELGIUM

Ruben **Dias**
PORTUGAL

Kevin **De Bruyne**
BELGIUM

Erling **Haaland**
NORWAY

Kylian **Mbappe**
FRANCE

Thibaut Courtois

NORTH & CENTRAL AMERICA

Keylor **Navas**
COSTA RICA

Alphonso **Davies**
CANADA

Tyler **Adams**
USA

Christian **Pulisic**
USA

Jonathan **David**
CANADA

Tyler Adams

SOUTH AMERICA

Alisson **Becker**
BRAZIL

Marquinhos
BRAZIL

Casemiro
BRAZIL

Lionel **Messi**
ARGENTINA

Vinicius **Junior**
BRAZIL

Casemiro

THE TEAMS RANKED!

Rank the five-a-side teams below in order — starting with the best continent and ending with the worst!

1 EUROPE

2 SOUTH AMERICA

3 AFRICA

4 NORTH & CENTRAL USA

5 ASIA

19

SPOT THE BALL!

We've removed the ball from the FOUR PREMIER LEAGUE PHOTOS below – can you guess where it should be?

BALL 1

ANSWER: E 2

BALL 2

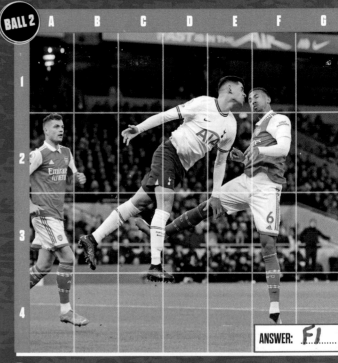

ANSWER: F1

BALL 3

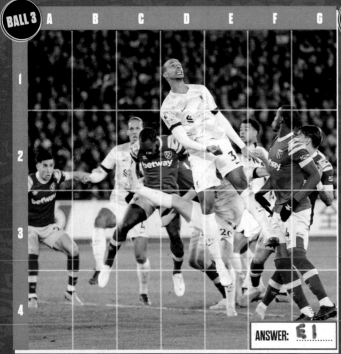

ANSWER: E1

BALL 4

ANSWER: D1

STADIUM SEARCH!

Can you find the 12 BRITISH FOOTBALL STADIUMS hiding in the word grid below?

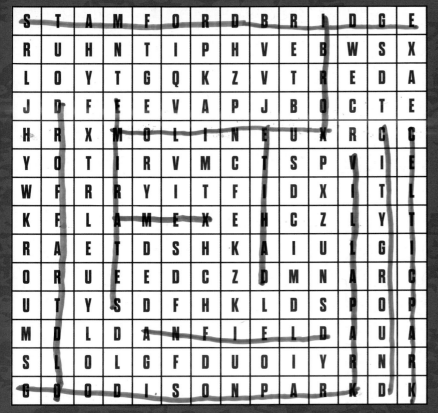

S	T	A	M	F	O	R	D	B	R	I	D	G	E
R	U	H	N	T	I	P	H	V	E	B	W	S	X
L	O	Y	T	G	Q	K	Z	V	T	R	E	D	A
J	D	F	E	E	V	A	P	J	B	O	C	T	E
H	R	X	M	O	L	I	N	E	U	X	R	C	C
Y	O	T	I	R	V	M	C	T	S	P	V	I	E
W	F	R	R	Y	I	T	F	I	D	X	I	T	L
K	F	L	A	M	E	X	E	H	C	Z	L	Y	T
R	A	E	T	D	S	H	K	A	I	U	L	G	I
O	R	U	E	E	D	C	Z	D	M	N	A	R	C
U	T	Y	S	D	F	H	K	L	D	S	P	O	P
M	D	L	D	A	N	F	I	E	L	D	A	U	A
S	L	O	L	G	F	D	U	O	I	Y	R	N	R
G	O	O	D	I	S	O	N	P	A	R	K	D	K

★ AMEX
★ ANFIELD
★ CELTIC PARK
★ CITY GROUND
★ EMIRATES
★ ETIHAD
★ GOODISON PARK
★ IBROX
★ MOLINEUX
★ OLD TRAFFORD
★ STAMFORD BRIDGE
★ VILLA PARK

GUESS WHO!

Name these high-profile FOOTY MANAGERS pictured in their playing days!

1 NAME: ?

2 NAME: PEP

3 NAME: ?

4 NAME: ?

ANSWERS ON PAGE 92!

WSL IN

32,262
The biggest stadium in the WSL is the King Power, home of Leicester's women's and men's teams!

2011
The Women's Super League was founded 12 years ago, replacing the old Premier League National as the top tier of women's football in England!

The first winners of the WSL were Arsenal!

12
The number of teams in the WSL — only Arsenal and Chelsea have played in every season!

6
Chelsea's title win last season was their sixth — meaning they've won the league twice as many times as their closest challengers, Arsenal!

WSL TITLE WINS
6 CHELSEA
3 ARSENAL
2 LIVERPOOL
1 MAN. CITY

£300K
Dutch baller Jill Roord became the WSL's most expensive player when she joined Man. City from German side Wolfsburg in July 2023. Midfielder Roord returns to the WSL after playing for Arsenal from 2019 to 2021!

NUMBERS!

42

Arsenal's Beth Mead is the top creator in WSL history — she's clocked up a total of 42 assists for the Gunners and previous club Sunderland!

78

Superstar striker Vivianne Miedema is the WSL's record goalscorer — she's bagged 78 goals in just 97 games since joining Arsenal in 2017!

MAGIC MIEDEMA!

Most WSL goals in a season: 22 in 2018-19

Most goals in a WSL match: 6 v Bristol City in 2019-20

Most WSL hat-tricks: 5

56

Man. United and England keeper Mary Earps has kept a record number of 56 clean sheets in her WSL career — 14 of those came last season as she won the Golden Glove!

16 years, 30 days

England star Lauren James became the youngest player in WSL history when she made her debut for Arsenal as a 16-year-old in 2017!

Arsenal 11 Bristol City 1

The biggest win in WSL history came in the 2019-20 season — with Netherlands ace Vivianne Miedema scoring six and assisting four of the 11 goals!

22

Lioness Rachel Daly netted 22 times for Aston Villa last season — meaning she shares the most goals in a season record with Miedema!

BBC
MATCH OF THE DAY
MAGAZINE

If you love footy, then you'll love Match of the Day magazine! 😃

+ Packed with the Prem's best ballers and global superstars!

+ Loaded with LOLs, quizzes, activities and epic posters!

+ Bursting with top skills advice, gaming tips and sick boot drops!

FUN-FILLED PAGES FOR YOUNG FOOTY FANS!

ON SALE EVERY FORTNIGHT!

No.1 MAG FOR WOMEN'S FOOTBALL!

And it tastes delicious!

RUBEN DIAS
PORTUGAL

BADGES & ANIMALS!

Welcome to my zoo!

Can you GUESS THE ENGLISH CLUBS simply by the animals that appear on their badges?

1
- A Tottenham
- B Bradford
- C Stoke ✔

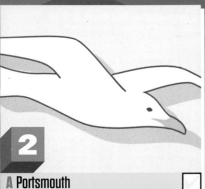

2
- A Portsmouth
- B Blackpool
- C Brighton ✔

3
- A Southampton
- B Derby ✔
- C Ipswich

4
- A Coventry
- B Reading
- C Wycombe ✔

5
- A West Brom
- B Sheffield Wednesday ✔
- C Wigan

6
- A Luton
- B Leicester
- C Hull ✔

7
- A Millwall
- B Crystal Palace ✔
- C Leeds

8
- A Watford
- B Brentford ✔
- C Bristol City

9
- A Preston
- B Huddersfield ✔
- C Burnley

YOUR FOOTY BRAIN POWER

YOUR SCORE ☐/9

9	GENIUS
7	PROFESSIONAL
5	SEMI-PRO
3	AMATEUR
1	SUNDAY LEAGUE
0	OH NO, DISASTER

ANSWERS ON PAGE 92!

27

GLOBAL FOOTY TOUR....

WITH ADAM LA LLAMA!

Pack your suitcase and join us as we travel around the great big world of football!

AFRICA

Countries 54 Area 30,370,000 km2
Total population 1.4 billion
Biggest city Cairo, Egypt
(population 20 million)

FOOTBALL IN AFRICA
FIFA confederation Confederation of African Football (CAF)
CAF HQ Egypt Formed 1957 Member countries 54

MOST SUCCESSFUL CLUB
AL AHLY, EGYPT
11 x African champions

THE SUPERSTAR
MOHAMED SALAH
EGYPT
Prolific, record-breaking
star who has obliterated
Prem and UCL defences
over the past six years!

MOST SUCCESSFUL NATION
EGYPT
7 x African champions

ADAM SAYS
Apparently, more than 2,000
different languages are spoken
across the continent. Mad!

THE LEGEND
SAMUEL ETO'O
CAMEROON
Won three La Liga titles,
three UCL trophies and
was African Footballer
of the Year FOUR times!

BIGGEST STADIUM
FNB STADIUM
Johannesburg, South Africa
94,736

ASIA

MOST SUCCESSFUL CLUB
AL-HILAL,
SAUDI ARABIA
4 x Asian champions

FOOTBALL IN ASIA
FIFA confederation Asian Football Confederation (AFC)
AFC HQ Malaysia Formed 1954 Member countries 47

MOST SUCCESSFUL NATION
JAPAN
4 x Asian champions

Countries 49 Area 44,579,000 km2
Total population 4.7 billion
Biggest city Tokyo, Japan
(population 38 million)

THE SUPERSTAR
SON HEUNG-MIN
SOUTH KOREA
Dynamic forward who is
the top Asian goalscorer
in both Premier League
and UCL history!

ADAM SAYS
Asia's most deadly
creature is not the tiger, snake
or crocodile — it's the mosquito!

THE LEGEND
ALI DAEI
IRAN
He was the world's top
international scorer with
109 goals, until Cristiano
Ronaldo broke his record!

BIGGEST STADIUM
RUNGRADO MAY
DAY STADIUM
Pyongyang, North Korea
114,000

EUROPE

Countries 50 Area 10,180,000 km2 Total population 742 million
Biggest city Istanbul, Turkey (population 15.8 million)

FOOTBALL IN EUROPE
FIFA confederation Union of European Football Associations (UEFA)
UEFA HQ Switzerland Formed 1954 Member countries 55

THE SUPERSTAR
KYLIAN MBAPPE
FRANCE
The French star looks set to dominate football for the next decade with his pace and fire finishing!

THE LEGEND
CRISTIANO RONALDO
PORTUGAL
Has scored more than 800 career goals, won five Ballons d'Or, five UCL titles and is international football's record goalscorer!

BIGGEST STADIUM
NOU CAMP
Barcelona, Spain
99,354

MOST SUCCESSFUL NATION
GERMANY
4 x World Cup winners
3 x Euros winners

ADAM SAYS
Almost 90 million tourists visit France each year, making it the world's most visited country! Zut alors!

MOST SUCCESSFUL CLUB
REAL MADRID, SPAIN
14 x European champions

NORTH AMERICA

Countries 23 Area 24,709,000 km2
Total population 604 million
Biggest city Mexico City, Mexico
(population 21.8 million)

**BIGGEST STADIUM
AZTEC STADIUM**
Mexico City, Mexico
87,523

THE SUPERSTAR
ALPHONSO DAVIES
CANADA
One of the quickest players around today, the left-back is vital for club and country in both defence and attack!

THE LEGEND
HUGO SANCHEZ
MEXICO
Famed for his acrobatic overhead kicks, he bagged 208 goals in 283 games for Spanish giants Real Madrid!

**MOST SUCCESSFUL CLUB |
CLUB AMERICA,
MEXICO**
7 x CONCACAF champions

**MOST SUCCESSFUL NATION
MEXICO**
11 x CONCACAF champions

ADAM SAYS
Americans love a burger — they munch through 50 BILLION every year. Wow!

FOOTBALL IN NORTH AMERICA
FIFA confederation Confederation of North, Central American And Caribbean Association Football (CONCACAF) CONCACAF HQ USA Formed 1961 Member countries 41

OCEANIA

FOOTBALL IN OCEANIA
FIFA confederation Oceania Football Confederation (OFC) OFC HQ New Zealand Formed 1966 Member countries 13

Countries 14 Area 8,526,000 km2
Total population 44 million
Biggest city Sydney, Australia
(population 5 million)

THE SUPERSTAR
MATHEW RYAN
AUSTRALIA
Having played at three World Cups, in La Liga and the Prem, the keeper is the current Australia captain!

THE LEGEND
TIM CAHILL
AUSTRALIA
The attacking midfielder is Australia's record goalscorer, after netting 50 goals in 108 games!

**MOST SUCCESSFUL CLUB
AUCKLAND CITY,
NEW ZEALAND**
7 x OFC champions

**MOST SUCCESSFUL NATION |
NEW ZEALAND**
5 x Oceania champions

ADAM SAYS
Australia quit the OFC in 2006 to join the Asian Confederation, for a better chance of qualifying for World Cups!

**BIGGEST STADIUM
STADIUM AUSTRALIA**
Sydney, Australia
83,500

SOUTH AMERICA

Countries 12 Area 17,840,000 km2
Total population 441 million
Biggest city Sao Paulo, Brazil
(population 22 million)

FOOTBALL IN SOUTH AMERICA
FIFA confederation South American Football Confederation (CONMEBOL)
CONMEBOL HQ Paraguay Formed 1916 Member countries 10

BIGGEST STADIUM
ESTADIO MONUMENTAL
Buenos Aires, Argentina
83,198

THE SUPERSTAR
LIONEL MESSI
ARGENTINA

Quite simply the Greatest Of All Time, the 36-year-old has won a record SEVEN Ballon d'Or awards, almost 40 club trophies and scored more than 800 career goals!

THE LEGEND
PELE *BRAZIL*

Legends don't get much bigger than footy's first superstar. The Brazilian baller scored more than 1,200 goals and won three World Cups — a record!

MOST SUCCESSFUL NATION
BRAZIL
5 x World Cup winners
9 x Copa America winners

MOST SUCCESSFUL CLUB
INDEPENDIENTE, ARGENTINA
7 x South American champions

ADAM SAYS
On Google it says in parts of South America, they eat llama... what? Eek! Taxi for me, I think!

33

NETHERLANDS

VAN DIJK

MATCH OF THE DAY MAGAZINE
WORLD DREAM TEAM!
CENTRE BACK

WOULD YOU RATHER...?

Grab a mate and tackle these SIX HUGE footballing dilemmas!

WIN THE WORLD CUP! OR **WIN £5 MILLION ON THE LOTTERY!**

BE A SQUAD PLAYER AT MAN. CITY! OR **BE A STAR PLAYER FOR BOURNEMOUTH!**

MISS A PENALTY IN A SHOOTOUT! OR **SCORE AN OWN GOAL IN A FINAL!**

HAVE A SAUSAGE ROLL FOR A NOSE! OR **HAVE HALF-TIME FRIES FOR HAIR!**

BE A PREMIER LEAGUE HERO! OR **BE A MARVEL SUPERHERO!**

BE A CAT BUT AMAZING AT FOOTBALL! OR **BE A HUMAN BUT RUBBISH AT FOOTBALL!**

YOUR AMAZING FOOTY CAREER!

Fill in the blank boxes to map out your epic footy journey from wonderkid to legend!

STEP 1

YOU'RE 14 YEARS OLD...

After starring for your school and junior team, your local Football League club scouts you and invites you to join their academy!

[WRITE YOUR CLOSEST EFL CLUB NAME HERE]

ABERDEEN

STEP 2

YOU MAKE YOUR EFL DEBUT AT 17...

And after three seasons of dazzling displays and media hype, your club accepts an £8m bid and you move to your nearest Premier League club!

[WRITE YOUR NEAREST PREM CLUB NAME HERE]

NEWCASTLE

STEP 3

AFTER TWO SENSATIONAL SEASONS...

You've put in sick performances every week, and you're linked with a big money move to a Prem giant. Every club wants you — choose any one you want!

[WRITE YOUR CHOSEN PREM CLUB NAME HERE]

MAN CITY

STEP 4

YOU'RE A STAR FOR CLUB & COUNTRY...

You're 28 and ready for a new challenge abroad. You are wanted by every UCL superclub in Europe — take your pick of which team to join in a mega £120m deal!

[WRITE YOUR CHOSEN UCL CLUB NAME HERE]

BARCA

STEP 5

YOU'RE A FOOTY ICON...

After four seasons of UCL and league success, and winning the Ballon d'Or twice, you're 32 years old and thinking about quitting elite level footy. You make a £20m move to a Europa League team!

[WRITE YOUR CHOSEN UEL CLUB NAME HERE]

BARCA

STEP 6

AFTER AN INJURY-HIT TWO SEASONS...

You're now 34 years old and starting to wind down your career. You decide to leave European footy and join an MLS team in the USA for a season!

[WRITE YOUR CHOSEN MLS CLUB NAME HERE]

INTER MIAMI

STEP 7

AFTER A CAREER OF SUCCESS...

You've won 100 caps, the UCL, several leagues titles and the Ballon d'Or — you decide to return for two final seasons with an EFL club before retiring!

[WRITE YOUR CHOSEN EFL CLUB NAME HERE]

MAN CITY

Alphonso

DavieS

Canada

CANADA

19

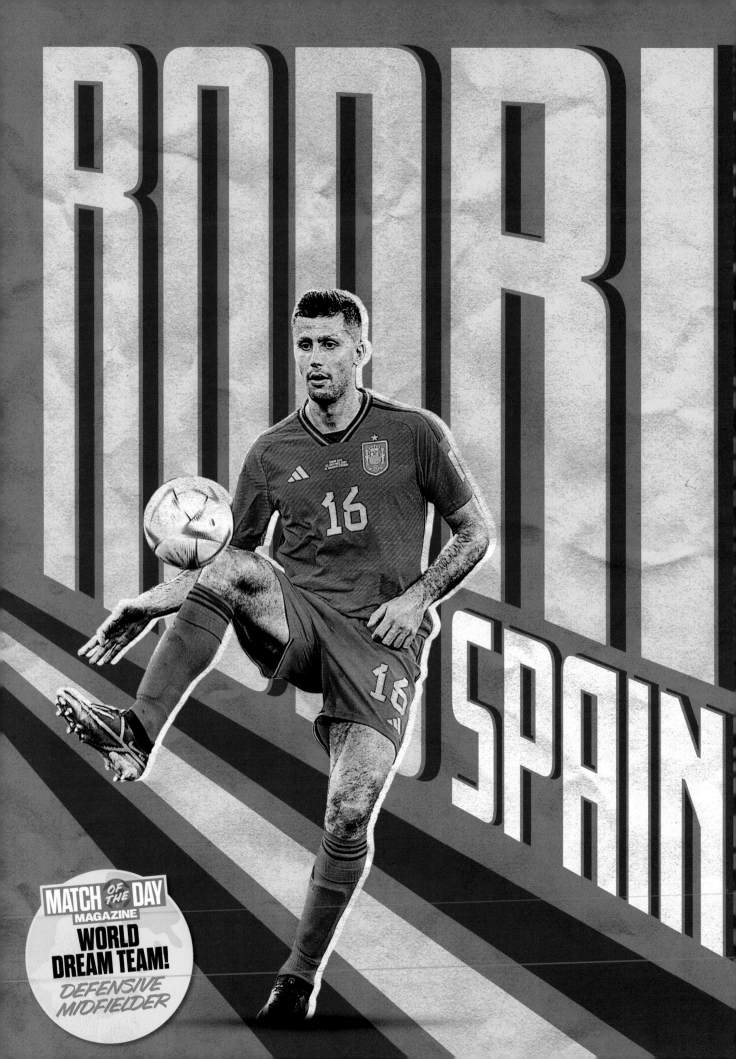

RODRI

SPAIN

MATCH OF THE DAY MAGAZINE

WORLD DREAM TEAM!

DEFENSIVE MIDFIELDER

A YEAR IN FOOTBALL!

How much can you remember about FOOTY IN 2023? It's time to find out!

1

Who won last season's EFL Cup back in February?

- A Newcastle
- B Man. City ✓
- C Man. United

2

What was the score in the 2022-23 FA Cup final?

- A Man. City 1-0 Man. United
- B Man. City 2-1 Man. United
- C Man. City 3-1 Man. United ✓

3

Who finished bottom of the Premier League last season?

- A Southampton ✓
- B Leicester
- C Leeds

4

Who was sacked as Everton boss back in January 2023?

- A Patrick Vieira
- B Frank Lampard ✓
- C Nathan Jones

5

Who did West Ham beat in the Europa Conference League final?

- A Sampdoria
- B Fiorentina ✓
- C AZ Alkmaar

6

Which club won La Liga last season?

- A Real Madrid
- B Barcelona ✓
- C Sevilla

7

Who scored the only goal of the game in the UCL final?

- A Erling Haaland
- B Rodri ✓
- C Ilkay Gundogan

8

Who was top scorer in the WSL last season?

- A Sam Kerr
- B Rachel Daly
- C Alessia Russo ✓

9

Who became Arsenal's record signing in July 2023?

- A Jurrien Timber
- B Kai Havertz
- C Declan Rice ✓

YOUR FOOTY BRAIN POWER

YOUR SCORE ☐/9	
9	GENIUS
7	PROFESSIONAL
5	SEMI-PRO
3	AMATEUR
1	SUNDAY LEAGUE
0	OH NO, DISASTER

ANSWERS ON PAGE 92!

39

+TOP TEN

GOALS TO SCORE!

From heroic headers to brilliant bicycle kicks, we count down the best types of goal before revealing our No.1!

+ THE ONE-ON-ONE!

10

You've timed your run to perfection and you're in on goal with only the keeper to beat. They're racing off their line to narrow the angle — time for deep breaths, a cool head and then either a) slot it low into the corner, b) dink it over them, or c) go round them!

THE MASTER: KYLIAN MBAPPE

DIFFICULTY RATING: 5/10

WOW FACTOR: 🔥🔥

SCORED IT! ✗

+ THE BULLET HEADER!

9

There are loads of different types of headers: glancing, cushioned, looping, diving — but our favourite is the thumping bullet header that rockets into the back of the net. It's all about a giant leap, a perfect connection and bulging neck muscles to get the power!

THE MASTER: HARRY KANE

DIFFICULTY RATING: 6/10

WOW FACTOR: 🔥🔥🔥

SCORED IT! ✓

+ THE TEAM GOAL!

8

This may end up being a simple tap-in from two yards out, but it's what has gone before that makes this special. Pep Guardiola teams are the kings of the pass-and-move and often make 30 passes or more before hitting the net. It takes all 11 players to be on the same page!

THE MASTER: MAN. CITY

DIFFICULTY RATING: 6/10

WOW FACTOR: 🔥🔥🔥🔥🔥

SCORED IT! ✔

+ THE CHEEKY CHIP!

7

This one is proof that a wondergoal doesn't have to be all about power. This delicate dink often flies through the air in slow motion, but all the back-peddling or wrong-footed keeper can do is watch it sail over them before it nestles in the back of the net!

THE MASTER: MOHAMED SALAH

DIFFICULTY RATING: 7/10

WOW FACTOR: 🔥🔥🔥🔥🔥

SCORED IT! ✔

+ THE PANENKA!

6

How can a penalty be one of the best goals you can score? Well, it's the King of Penalties. Named after Antonin Panenka, who did this pen for the first time at Euro '76, this is about faking you're going to blast it into the corner, but instead delicately dink it down the middle!

THE MASTER: KARIM BENZEMA

DIFFICULTY RATING: 8/10

WOW FACTOR: 🔥🔥🔥🔥🔥

SCORED IT! ✓

+ THE TOP BINS BOMB!

5

Goals from outside the box come in all shapes and sizes, and nothing looks more spectacular than hitting top bins from 30 yards out. This requires great technique, accuracy and a super-charged boot to make sure it fizzes into the top corner past the despairing keeper!

THE MASTER: KEVIN DE BRUYNE

DIFFICULTY RATING: 8/10

WOW FACTOR: 🔥🔥🔥🔥🔥

SCORED IT! ✓

+ THE SICK FREE-KICK!

4

Bending a 25-yard free-kick into the top corner is one of football's greatest sights, but it's pretty rare to see. Getting the ball up and over a five-man wall is harder than it looks. You need concentration and technique to find the perfect balance of accuracy and power!

THE MASTER: MARCUS RASHFORD

DIFFICULTY RATING: 8/10

WOW FACTOR: 🔥🔥🔥🔥🔥

SCORED IT! ✓

+ THE HUGE VOLLEY!

3

Another glorious sight, and one which leaves fans in awe. This requires unbelievable tekkers and co-ordination to ensure there's a clean connection and that the ball doesn't go flying over the bar. Always a goal of the season contender if executed to perfection!

THE MASTER: ROBERT LEWANDOWSKI

DIFFICULTY RATING: 8/10

WOW FACTOR: 🔥🔥🔥🔥🔥

SCORED IT! ✓

+ THE SOLO DRIBBLE!

2

■ A feint, a stepover, a side-step, a burst of acceleration, a shimmy, another stepover, another feint, a nutmeg and then a cool-as-you-like side-foot into the far corner... wow. The mazy dribble followed by a clinical finish is so tough, and that's what makes it so special!

THE MASTER: LIONEL MESSI

DIFFICULTY RATING: 9/10

WOW FACTOR: 🔥🔥🔥🔥🔥

SCORED IT! ✓

+ THE OVERHEAD KICK!

1

■ This is the goal that everyone dreams of scoring! The acrobatic overhead kick should be framed and put in an art gallery — it's a thing of beauty. As the player leaps into the air, time stops before... BOOM the connection and then the ball rockets past the helpless keeper!

THE MASTER: ERLING HAALAND

DIFFICULTY RATING: 10/10

WOW FACTOR: 🔥🔥🔥🔥🔥

SCORED IT! ✓

JUDE
BELLINGHAM

ENGLAND

22

MAKE FOOTBALL EVERYONE'S GAME

MATCH OF THE DAY
MAGAZINE
WORLD
DREAM TEAM!
MIDFIELDER

BIG MONEY MEN!

 Jackpot!

Which player holds the record for being his country's MOST EXPENSIVE ever transfer?

ARGENTINA

1
- **A** Lionel Messi ✔
- **B** Enzo Fernandez
- **C** Lautaro Martinez

PORTUGAL

2
- **A** Luis Figo
- **B** Cristiano Ronaldo ✔
- **C** Joao Felix

ITALY

3
- **A** Roberto Baggio
- **B** Sandro Tonali
- **C** Jorginho ✔

NETHERLANDS

4
- **A** Frenkie de Jong
- **B** Virgil van Dijk
- **C** Arjen Robben ✔

GERMANY

5
- **A** Kai Havertz
- **B** Ilkay Gundogan ✔
- **C** Joshua Kimmich

SCOTLAND

6
- **A** John McGinn
- **B** Andy Robertson ✔
- **C** Kieran Tierney

NORWAY

7
- **A** Erling Haaland ✔
- **B** Martin Odegaard
- **C** Sander Berge

SPAIN

8
- **A** Andres Iniesta ✔
- **B** Kepa Arrizabalaga
- **C** Rodri

SOUTH KOREA

9
- **A** Son Heung-min ✔
- **B** Kim Min-jae
- **C** Park Ji-sung

YOUR FOOTY BRAIN POWER

YOUR SCORE ⬜/9	9	GENIUS
	7	PROFESSIONAL
	5	SEMI-PRO
	3	AMATEUR
	1	SUNDAY LEAGUE
	0	OH NO, DISASTER

ANSWERS ON PAGE 92!

47

BARCELONA
LA LIGA CHAMPIONS

2022-23

NAPOLI
SERIE A
CHAMPIONS

CHELSEA
WSL CHAMPIONS

PSG
LIGUE 1 CHAMPIONS

CELTIC
SCOTTISH PREMIERSHIP
CHAMPIONS

AGUE
NERS

BAYERN MUNICH
BUNDESLIGA CHAMPIONS

49

YOU ARE A...

SUPERSTAR BALLER!

How would YOU spend £500m on your dream superstar life — it's time to make some BIG decisions!

NAME: Freddie Irwin
AGE: 10 **NICKNAME:** Fred
HEIGHT: 5'9 **WEIGHT:** 172 Lbs
POSITION: Attacking MID

SIGNATURE: Irwin

Stick your photo here and fill in your baller fact file!

Give yourself a sick autograph!

WHAT YOU NEED TO DO!

1 Work through the 11 sections over the next seven pages.

2 Choose ONE option for each category.

3 You can't go over your £500m budget, so keep a note of how much you're spending.

4 When you've made your choices, cut them out and stick them into the correct place on p60-61.

ASK AN ADULT TO HELP YOU WITH THE CUTTING!

① THE STADIUM
Which ground do you want to play in?

TOTTENHAM HOTSPUR STADIUM ✔
CAPACITY **62,850** PRICE **£50m**

THE AMEX
CAPACITY **31,800** PRICE **£30m**

KENILWORTH ROAD
CAPACITY **10,356** PRICE **£10m**

② THE CLUB
Which team are you going to sign for?

REAL MADRID PRICE **£50m** ✔

MAN. UNITED PRICE **£40m**

NAPOLI PRICE **£30m**

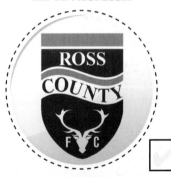

INTER MIAMI PRICE **£20m**

PETERBOROUGH PRICE **£10m**

ROSS COUNTY PRICE **£5m**

③ THE MANAGER
Which boss do you want to play under?

PEP GUARDIOLA PRICE **£60m** ✔

MIKEL ARTETA PRICE **£40m**

EDDIE HOWE PRICE **£30m**

DAVID MOYES PRICE **£10m**

NEIL WARNOCK PRICE **£5m**

SPENT SO FAR!
£160.M.

Use a calculator to add up your spending as you go along!

BALLER LIFE

MOHAMED SALAH

Mo, who is sponsored by brands like Adidas, Pepsi and Uber, has made huge donations to improve the lives of people in Egypt!

BALLER LIFE

ROBERT LEWANDOWSKI

Nike athlete and FIFA cover star Lewy has donated and raised money for loads of charitable organisations throughout his career!

④ YOUR SQUAD

Time to assemble your awesome crew!

SUPERSTAR TEAM-MATE

LIONEL MESSI ✓
PRICE £60m

CRISTIANO RONALDO ☐
PRICE £50m

KYLIAN MBAPPE ☐
PRICE £40m

NEYMAR ☐
PRICE £30m

ROBERT LEWANDOWSKI ☐
PRICE £20m

HERO STRIKER

ERLING HAALAND ✓
PRICE £60m

HARRY KANE ☐
PRICE £50m

MARCUS RASHFORD ☐
PRICE £40m

ALEXANDER ISAK ☐
PRICE £30m

OLLIE WATKINS ☐
PRICE £20m

BEST MATE

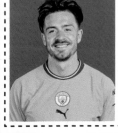

JACK GREALISH ✓
PRICE £60m

BUKAYO SAKA ☐
PRICE £50m

JUDE BELLINGHAM ☐
PRICE £40m

MASON MOUNT ☐
PRICE £30m

JORDAN PICKFORD ☐
PRICE £20m

⑤ THE PET

Which animal will you choose to hang with?

DOG ☐
PRICE £30m

CAT ✓
PRICE £20m

HAMSTER ☐
PRICE £10m

GOLDFISH ☐
PRICE £5m

SPENT SO FAR!
£370.M

Use a calculator to add up your spending as you go along!

BALLER LIFE
MARCUS RASHFORD
Rashy's high-profile campaigning and donations have helped combat homelessness, child food poverty and improve literacy!

BALLER LIFE
KYLIAN MBAPPE
Kyl brings in millions from deals with Nike, Hublot and Oakley, but he's also donated millions to good causes during that time!

6 THE SHIRT NUMBER
Pick your squad number for the season!

NO.10 PRICE £50m		NO.7 PRICE £30m ✓	NO.18 PRICE £20m	NO.32 PRICE £10m

7 THE CAR
Choose the whip you'll ride around in!

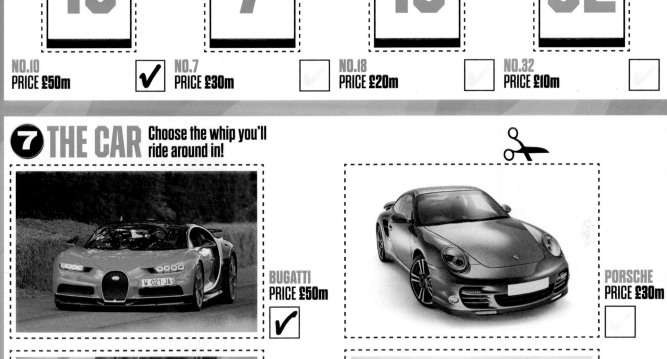

BUGATTI PRICE £50m ✓

PORSCHE PRICE £30m

HONDA PRICE £20m ✓

MINI PRICE £10m ✓

8 THE HOUSE
Select where you're going to chill after games!

MANSION PRICE £50m	MODERN PRICE £40m ✓	BUNGALOW PRICE £20m	CARAVAN PRICE £10m

SPENT SO FAR!
£ 510 M

Use a calculator to add up your spending as you go along!

★
BALLER LIFE
HARRY KANE
Harry launched the Harry Kane Foundation in 2022 to help change people's out-dated thinking about mental health!

★
BALLER LIFE
BUKAYO SAKA
Saka earns loads from his boot deal, but he's also happy giving to charity. Last year he funded 120 life-changing operations!

⑨ THE SPONSORSHIP
Which big-money deal are you going to accept?

EA FC COVER STAR
PRICE £50m ✓

ODEON INFLUENCER
PRICE £30m ✓

FACE OF CLARKS SHOES
PRICE £20m ✓

GREGGS AMBASSADOR
PRICE £10m ✓

⑩ THE BOOT DEAL
Pick the wheels that you'll ball in!

NIKE
PRICE £50m ☐

PUMA
PRICE £30m ✓

UMBRO
PRICE £20m ☐

CONCAVE
PRICE £10m ✓

⑪ THE CHARITY DONATION
How much money will you give to good causes?

HUGE DONATION
PRICE £50m ☐

DECENT DONATION
PRICE £40m ✓

SMALL DONATION
PRICE £20m ✓

TINY DONATION
PRICE £10m ✓

SPENT SO FAR!
£630.M

Use a calculator to add up your spending as you go along!

⭐
BALLER LIFE
LIONEL MESSI
Leo has sponsorship deals with Adidas, Pepsi and Mastercard. He's a UNICEF ambassador and has his own charitable foundation!

⭐
BALLER LIFE
CRISTIANO RONALDO
CR7 is a multi-million pound brand, he's Nike's A-list athlete and he's donated millions to charity during his 20-year career!

★
BALLER LIFE
NEYMAR
Ney makes millions from 35 sponsorship deals, but he also gives back as his Neymar Jr. Institute provides help to vulnerable children in Brazil!

★
BALLER LIFE
JACK GREALISH
The £100 million man, who has deals with Puma and Gucci, gives loads to good causes, including local hospitals and poorly fans!

+ MY BALLER LIFE +

You've made your choices, now it's time to glue your selections in place and put your new pro baller lifestyle together!

SPURS STADIUM

YOUR STADIUM

REAL MADRIO

YOUR CLUB

Stick your baller fact file here!

PEY

YOUR SQUAD

YOUR MANAGER

Slurp!

SUPERSTAR TEAM-MATE	HERO STRIKER	BEST MATE
MESS	HAILANI	Grealish

DOG

YOUR
PET

YOUR
SHIRT
NUMBER

10

YOUR
CAR

YOUR
HOUSE

YOUR
SPONSOR

YOUR
BOOTS

FINAL
SPEND!
£ 630 M

YOUR
CHARITY
DONATION

20

THINGS YOU NEED TO KNOW ABOUT

EURO 2024!

The ultimate guide to next summer's huge tournament!

1

IT'S BEING HELD IN GERMANY!

Yep, Germany will host Euro 2024, the 17th European Championship. The Euros were held in West Germany in 1988, but this will be the first time the country has staged the Euros since reunification!

HISTORY LESSON!

Between 1949 and 1990, Germany was divided into two countries — West Germany and East Germany.

2 WHEN IS EURO 2024?

14

The tournament will last a whole month and takes place from 14 June to 14 July 2024. Berlin will host the final on Sunday 14 July 2024, while the tourney kicks off in Munich on Friday 14 June!

THERE ARE 10 HOST CITIES! 3

Ten amazing stadiums will be hosting games at Euro 2024. These venues are:

BERLIN
Olympiastadion
70,000

COLOGNE
Cologne Stadium
47,000

DORTMUND
BVB Stadion
66,000

DUSSELDORF
Dusseldorf Arena
47,000

FRANKFURT
Frankfurt Arena
46,000

GELSENKIRCHEN
Arena AufSchalke
50,000

HAMBURG
Volksparkstadion
50,000

LEIPZIG
Leipzig Stadium
42,000

MUNICH
Munich Football Arena
67,000

STUTTGART
Stuttgart Arena
54,000

4 SO HOW MANY TEAMS WILL BE THERE?

In total, 24 teams will take part. Germany qualify as hosts, 20 nations will earn their place at the finals via the qualification group stage and three more will join through the playoffs!

HOW WILL IT WORK? 5

There will be six groups, with the top two in each group qualifying for the knockout stage, along with the four best third-placed finishers!

9
UNITED BY FOOTBALL!

The tournament's official slogan is: 'United by Football. Vereint im Herzen Europas'. For those who don't speak German, the second part of the slogan is: 'United in the heart of Europe!'

6
BRING ON BERLIN!

The Euro 2024 final will be held at Berlin's Olympiastadion, Germany's biggest stadium. It hosted the 2006 World Cup final, the 2015 Champions League final and is the home of Hertha Berlin, who were relegated from the Bundesliga last season!

10
FRANCE SHOULD WIN IT!

France have already been named as the team to beat. After their epic penalty shootout defeat to Argentina in last year's World Cup final in Qatar, Kylian Mbappe and his mates will want to prove they're Europe's No.1!

MEET THE MASCOT!

The official mascot for Euro 2024 is a bear called Albart! Over the years, tournament mascots have included a rabbit called Berni, a lion named Goliath and a cockerel called Peno — but this is the first bear!

8
ITALY ARE THE REIGNING CHAMPS!

Who can forget the Euro 2020 final? England versus Italy, Wembley Stadium, the hosts dreaming of their first trophy since 1966 — but it was the Italians who won it thanks to a dramatic 3-2 penalty shootout!

7

11

EURO KINGS!

Germany and Spain are the two most successful nations in Euros history, both winning the title three times. In fact, ten countries have won the European Championship since it was introduced in 1960!

TEAM	WINS
GERMANY	3 (1972, 1980, 1996)
SPAIN	3 (1964, 2008, 2012)
ITALY	2 (1968, 2020)
FRANCE	2 (1984, 2000)
RUSSIA	1 (1960)
CZECH REPUBLIC	1 (1976)
PORTUGAL	1 (2016)
NETHERLANDS	1 (1988)
DENMARK	1 (1992)
GREECE	1 (2004)

12

MUNICH OPENER!

The Munich Football Arena, home to Bayern Munich, will host the opening ceremony and the first match of Euro 2024. Almost 70,000 fans will be packed into the iconic stadium for the tournament's kick-off, which will feature host nation Germany!

TALE OF THE TROPHY!

13 The Henri Delaunay trophy, which is awarded to the winner of the European Championships, is named after, well, Henri Delaunay. Henners was the first General Secretary of UEFA and the bloke who came up with the idea for the tournament!

The trophy weighs 8kg and is 60cm tall — the same height and weight as a Rhesus monkey!

GOLDEN BOOT!

As ever, the race for the Golden Boot promises to be sensational. Some of Europe's hottest strikers will go head-to-head in Germany next summer, but can any of them better French legend Michel Platini's tournament record? His nine goals at Euro 84 fired France to glory on home soil!

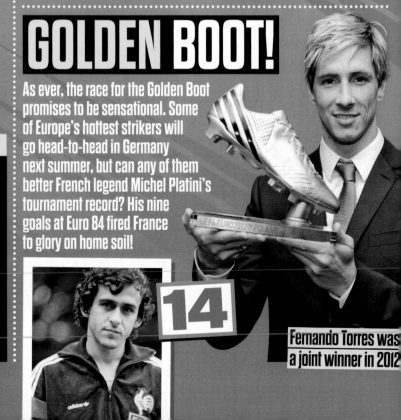

14

Fernando Torres was a joint winner in 2012

15

SCOTLAND EXPECTS!

Scotland failed to win a single game at the last Euros, although they did hold England to a 0-0 draw at Wembley. The Tartan Army have NEVER made it out of the group stage at a European Championship — can Steve Clarke's lads finally end that dismal record in Germany next summer?

16

THE EUROS GOAT!

Portugal superstar Cristiano Ronaldo holds a ridiculous number of European Championship records. He made his Euros debut in 2004 — and he hasn't looked back!

RONALDO'S RECORDS!	
Most tournaments	5 (2004, 2008, 2012, 2016, 2020)
Most matches played	25
Most matches won	12
Most goals scored	14

17

WORLD CUP MEMS!

The last time a football tournament was held in Germany was the 2006 World Cup, 18 years ago — and it was pure drama. England crashed out on penalties to Portugal in the quarter-finals, and France suffered penalty heartbreak in the final as Zinedine Zidane was sent off before they lost their shootout to Italy!

18

HOME SWEET HOME!

On the 12 occasions a Euros has been staged in a single country, the hosts have always made at least the semis, and have gone on to win it three times — Spain (1964), Italy (1968) and France (1984). Will Germany add their name to that list next summer?

GERMAN BANGERS!

19

If you love a sausage, this is the Euros for you. Germany is home to around 1,200 different types of banger, including the Bratwurst, Frankfurter, Weisswurst and Wollwurst!

20

ENGLAND'S DREAM OR NIGHTMARE!

Gareth Southgate's team were a penalty kick away from winning Euro 2020, but it wasn't to be. This will be their 11th Euros and they go into it as one of the favourites. One note of caution, though — the last time the Three Lions played in the Euros on German soil, at Euro 88, they lost every game!

TOP TRUMPS!

BOTTOM

BONKERS BADGES EDITION!

AVENIR BEGGEN
LUXEMBOURG

Club founded	1915
Bearded pixies	1
Footballs	1
Weirdness	79%
Rubbishness	65%
Cool factor	65%
BONKERS RATING	**88%**

DID YOU KNOW?
Avenir Beggen's nickname is Wichtelcher, which translates as the Pixies. These creatures are small and mischievous and known for playing tricks on people!

Is that a goblin?

AVENIR SPORTIF DE LA MARSA
TUNISIA

Club founded	1939
Bendy camels	1
Footballs	1
Weirdness	76%
Rubbishness	66%
Cool factor	43%
BONKERS RATING	**76%**

DID YOU KNOW?
Arabian camels can smell water from about 50 miles away — which can come in pretty handy if you're trudging through the desert with a massive thirst on!

CHANGCHUN YATAI FC
CHINA

Club founded	1996
Ducks with antlers	1
Footballs	1
Weirdness	88%
Rubbishness	46%
Cool factor	48%
BONKERS RATING	**89%**

DID YOU KNOW?
Changchun Yatai won the Chinese Super League by just a single point back in 2007, but the club from north-east China have failed to hit those heights since!

ARAGUAINA

ARAGUA... E REGATAS

BRAZIL

O TOURÃO DO NORTE

Club founded	1997
Confused cows	1
Canoes	1
Weirdness	89%
Rubbishness	88%
Cool factor	28%
BONKERS RATING	**86%**

DID YOU KNOW?

Araguaina is in rural Brazil, and is famous for cattle farming. The club's nickname 'Tourão do Norte' translates as 'The Big Bull of the North'. And they love a canoe!

ASFA YENNENGA

BURKINA FASO

ASFA - YENNENGA

Club founded	1947
White horses	1
Bow and arrows	1
Weirdness	79%
Rubbishness	56%
Cool factor	33%
BONKERS RATING	**62%**

DID YOU KNOW?

According to Burkina Faso folklore, Yennenga was a legendary warrior princess, who lived over 900 years ago. Loads of statues of her can be found in the country's capital!

AS PONTA LESTE

EAST TIMOR

Club founded	1991
Friendly crocodiles	1
Footballs	1
Weirdness	65%
Rubbishness	69%
Cool factor	22%
BONKERS RATING	**70%**

DID YOU KNOW?

East Timor, also known as Timor-Leste, is an island 400 miles north of Australia — and according to local legend, the island was formed out of a giant crocodile!

COBRESAL

CHILE

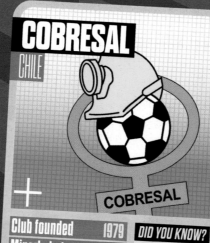

COBRESAL

Club founded	1979
Miner's hats	1
Footballs	1
Weirdness	72%
Rubbishness	76%
Cool factor	38%
BONKERS RATING	**71%**

DID YOU KNOW?

The club is based in El Salvador, a mining town in Chile. It's in the middle of the Atacama Desert, parts of which have NEVER had any rain!

CHICKEN INN FC

ZIMBABWE

Chicken Inn FC

Club founded	1997
Chickens	1
Footballs	1
Weirdness	55%
Rubbishness	70%
Cool factor	40%
BONKERS RATING	**59%**

DID YOU KNOW?

The club comes from Bulawayo, Zimbabwe's second largest city — but gets its unusual name from a fast-food restaurant, whose slogan is: Luv dat chicken!

WHO'S YOUR

LIONEL

MESSI

OR

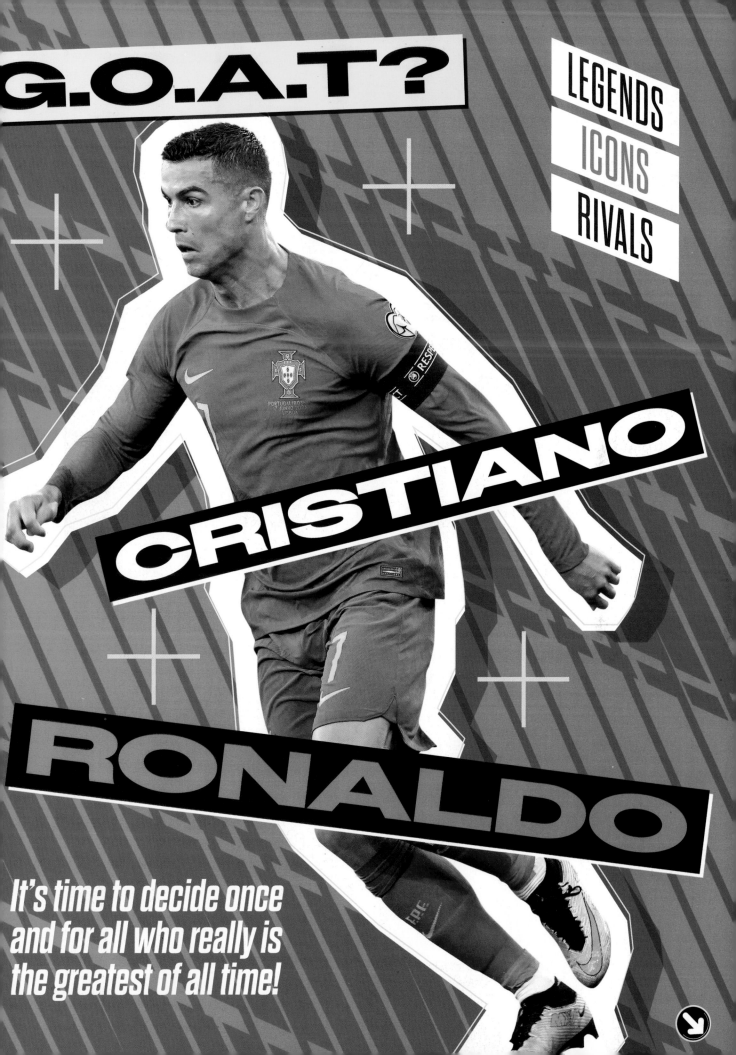

G.O.A.T?

LEGENDS
ICONS
RIVALS

CRISTIANO
RONALDO

It's time to decide once and for all who really is the greatest of all time!

He exploded onto the scene 20 years ago. He's won more Ballons d'Or than anyone. He's a legend at Barcelona and led his nation to World Cup glory last year. He is..

LIONEL MESSI

BORN 1987 AGE 36

BIRTHPLACE
ROSARIO
ARGENTINA

MAJOR TROPHIES

- **1** World Cup
- **1** Copa America
- **4** Champions League
- **10** La Liga
- **2** Ligue I
- **7** Copa del Rey
- **3** FIFA Club World Cup
- **3** UEFA Super Cup

TOTAL TROPHIES
40

PRO DEBUT: 2004

CLUB	COUNTRY
855	**175**
GAMES	GAMES
707	**103**
GOALS	GOALS

TOTAL
1,030 GAMES 810 GOALS
1 GOAL EVERY 1.27 GAMES

CAREER HIGHLIGHT WINNING THE 2022 WORLD CUP

FCB
2004-21
672 GOALS

PARIS SAINT-GERMAIN
2021-23
32 GOALS

CLUB INTERNACIONAL DE FUTBOL MIAMI MMXX
2023-
3 GOALS

*stats correct up to 1 Aug 2023

7

GOLDEN BOOTS

6 European
Golden shoes
6 Champions
League top scorer
8 La Liga top scorer
1 Copa America
top scorer

Does Messi's World Cup win in 2022 prove once and for all he's the GOAT?

BEST 5 SEASONS

1	2011-12	73 goals / 60 games
2	2012-13	60 goals / 50 games
3	2014-15	58 goals / 57 games
4	2016-17	54 goals / 52 games
5	2010-11	53 goals / 55 games

40+ GOALS IN A SEASON

10 TIMES

MESSI'S TOP 3 RECORDS

- Won a record 7 Ballon d'Or awards
- La Liga all-time record goalscorer
- Argentina all-time record goalscorer

I'M TEAM MESSI ☑

He's football's all-time record goalscorer. He's netted more goals at club level and international level than anyone in the history of the game. He's a born winner; he is..

CRISTIANO RONALDO

BORN 1985 AGE 38

BIRTHPLACE
FUNCHAL,
MADEIRA,
PORTUGAL

MAJOR TROPHIES

1 European Championship
1 UEFA Nations League
5 Champions League
3 Premier League
2 La Liga 2 Serie A
1 FA Cup 2 Copa del Rey
2 EFL Cup 1 Coppa Italia
4 FIFA Club World Cup
2 UEFA Super Cup

TOTAL TROPHIES
32

PRO DEBUT: 2002

CLUB	COUNTRY
968	**200**
GAMES	GAMES
715	**123**
GOALS	GOALS

TOTAL
1,168 GAMES **838** GOALS
1 GOAL EVERY **1.39** GAMES

CAREER HIGHLIGHT
WINNING A FIFTH
UCL TITLE IN 2018

2002-03
5 GOALS

2003-09
118 GOALS

2009-18
450 GOALS

JUVENTUS
2018-21
101 GOALS

2021-23
27 GOALS

2023-
14 GOALS

*stats correct up to 1 Aug 2023

Does Ronaldo's better goalscoring record mean he's No.1?

BALLON D'OR AWARDS

5

GOLDEN BOOTS

4 European Golden Shoes
7 Champions League top scorer
3 La Liga top scorer
1 Premier League top scorer
1 Serie A top scorer
2 European Championship top scorer

BEST 5 SEASONS

1	2014-15		61 goals / 54 games
2	2011-12		60 goals / 55 games
3	2012-13		55 goals / 55 games
4	2010-11		53 goals / 54 games
5	2013-14		51 goals / 47 games

40+ GOALS IN A SEASON

9 TIMES

RONALDO'S TOP 3 RECORDS

■ International football all-time record goalscorer
■ Champions League all-time record goalscorer
■ Real Madrid all-time record goalscorer

I'M TEAM RONALDO ✔

KEVIN DE BRUYNE

BELGIUM

MATCH OF THE DAY MAGAZINE
WORLD DREAM TEAM!
MIDFIELDER

QUIZ AN ADULT!

This is your chance to see just how much your chosen adult knows about football. Are they a genuine footy brainiac, or will they crumble under the pressure? LET'S FIND OUT!

BEFORE YOU START!

YOUR ADULT WILL NEED...

☑ A CUP OF TEA (MAYBE EVEN A BISCUIT)

☑ A FULLY FUNCTIONING FOOTY MEMORY

☑ THEIR FAVE SLIPPERS

☑ A PEN

NOW IT'S YOUR TURN TO BE QUIZ MASTER!

HAND·HELD CELL PHONE USE PROHIBITED

NO CHEATING! Put that phone away!

QUIZ AN ADULT!

QUIZ

1 MATCH THE AWESOME FOOTY STADIUMS TO THE CORRECT BADGE!

A ....

B ....

C ....

D ....

2 NAME THESE FIVE PREMIER LEAGUE PLAYERS FROM THE 1990S!

A ....

B ....

C ....

D ....

E ....

3 HE'S THE LAST ENGLISH BOSS TO WIN THE LEAGUE TITLE – BUT WHAT'S HIS NAME?

4 WHICH CLUBS WORE THESE ICONIC SHIRTS BACK IN THE DAY?

A ....

B ....

C ....

5 WHICH PREM CLUB DID THESE FOUR GAFFERS ALL MANAGE IN THE 1990S?

QUIZ

6
WHICH CLUBS WERE THESE PREMIER LEAGUE TOP SCORERS PLAYING FOR AT THE TIME THEY WON THE GOLDEN BOOT?

A ....

B ....

C ....

D ....

E ....

ANSWERS ON PAGE 92!

8
THIS GUY WAS NAMED IN THE PFA TEAM OF THE YEAR IN 1995-96. WHO IS HE?

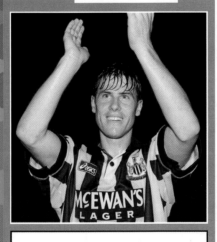

....

9
NAME THIS ARGENTINIAN PLAYMAKER WHO JOINED MAN. UNITED IN 2001.

....

7
ED DE GOEY WAS IN GOAL FOR WHICH CLUB IN THE 2000 FA CUP FINAL?

....

10
THIS STRIKER WAS PFA PLAYER OF THE YEAR AND TOP SCORER IN 1987. WHAT'S HIS NAME?

....

HALF-TIME
SCORE
☐ /23

QUIZ AN ADULT!

QUIZ

ANSWERS ON PAGE 92!

11

THIS GUY WAS TOP SCORER AT THE 1998 WORLD CUP. WHAT'S HIS NAME?

A Milan Baros

B Davor Suker

C Predrag Mijatovic

D Hristo Stoichkov

12

WHO BEAT ARSENAL 2-1 IN THE 2006 CHAMPIONS LEAGUE FINAL?

A Real Madrid

B Barcelona

C AC Milan

D Chelsea

13

WHICH COUNTRY DID AWESOME STRIKER SONNY ANDERSON PLAY FOR?

A South Africa

B Sweden

C Brazil

D Denmark

14

WHAT WAS THE NAME OF THIS ICONIC WORLD CUP MASCOT?

A Goalio

B Ciao

C Calcio

D Bravo

15

WHICH OF THESE PLAYERS DID NOT SCORE AT THE 2002 WORLD CUP?

A Sol Campbell

B Rio Ferdinand

C Emile Heskey

D Paul Scholes

16 WHO SCORED THE WINNER IN THE EURO 2008 FINAL?

| A David Villa | B Andres Iniesta |
| C Fernando Torres | D Cesc Fabregas |

17 WHICH COUNTRY WON THE 2004 EUROPEAN CHAMPIONSHIP?

A Portugal   B Denmark   C Greece   D France

18 WHO MANAGED ENGLAND AT EURO 2000?

A Glenn Hoddle   B Terry Venables   C Kevin Keegan   D Sven-Goran Eriksson

19 WHICH CLUB HAS NEVER WON THE CHAMPIONS LEAGUE?

A Porto   B Dortmund   C Marseille   D Atletico Madrid

20 WHICH 1998 WORLD CUP WINNER NEVER PLAYED IN THE PREM?

A Bixente Lizarazu   B Christian Karembeu   C Christophe Dugarry   D Youri Djorkaeff

How did you do?

FULL-TIME SCORE /33

81

NEVER MISS AN ISSUE OF

BBC

MATCH OF THE DAY
+ MAGAZINE

OFFER DEADLINE DATE
31 AUGUST 2024

◆ **PAY ONLY £4** *for your first four issues!*

◆ **CONTINUE TO SAVE 10%*** *after your trial!*

◆ **DELIVERY** *direct to your door every issue!*

◆ **NEVER MISS AN ISSUE** *of your favourite footy mag!*

SUBSCRIBE TODAY

VISIT buysubscriptions.com/MDPSANN23

CALL 03330 162 126† QUOTE MDPSANN23

VINICIUS JR
BRAZIL

MATCH OF THE DAY MAGAZINE
WORLD DREAM TEAM!
FORWARD

WHO THE HECK ARE YOU?

Llama chop!

Can you guess the HIDDEN BALLERS in the photos below?

1
....

2

KANE

3
....

4

BOWEN

5

HAALAND

6

PICKFORD

7

RUSSO

8

ANTONY

9
....

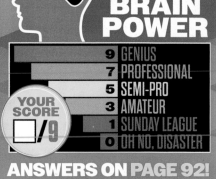

YOUR FOOTY BRAIN POWER

Score	Rank
9	GENIUS
7	PROFESSIONAL
5	SEMI-PRO
3	AMATEUR
1	SUNDAY LEAGUE
0	OH NO, DISASTER

YOUR SCORE ☐ /9

ANSWERS ON PAGE 92!

KYLIAN MBAPPE

MATCH OF THE DAY MAGAZINE
WORLD DREAM TEAM!
FORWARD

THE BEST OF THE BEST!

We collect stickers, Alexia Putellas collects trophies!

We reveal the top 30 players in women's football — does *YOUR* hero make our list?

1

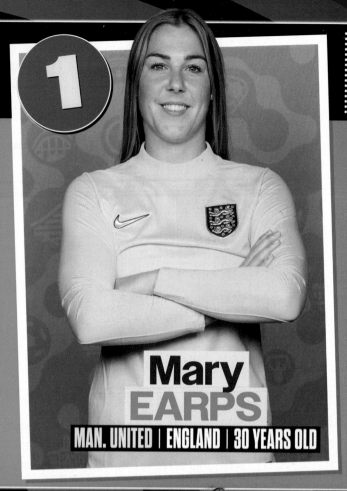

Mary
EARPS
MAN. UNITED | ENGLAND | 30 YEARS OLD

KEEPERS
→ Agile, commanding and brave
→ Expert decision maker with perfect passing
→ Intelligent, aware, with lightning reflexes

2

Merle FROHMS
WOLFSBURG | GERMANY | 28 YEARS OLD

3

Christine ENDLER
LYON | CHILE | 32 YEARS OLD

4

Sandra PANOS
BARCELONA | SPAIN | 30 YEARS OLD

5

Ann-Katrin BERGER
CHELSEA | GERMANY | 32 YEARS OLD

1

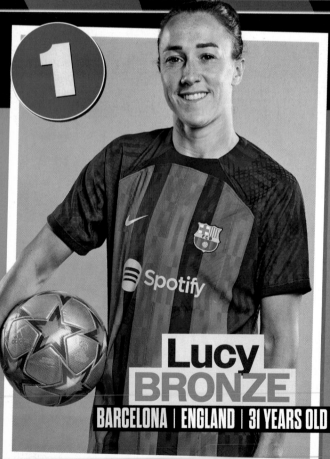

Lucy
BRONZE
BARCELONA | ENGLAND | 31 YEARS OLD

FULL-BACKS
→ Energetic, quick and super-fit
→ Excellent dribbling, passing and crossing skills
→ Tactically aware with positional intelligence

2

Fridolina ROLFO
BARCELONA | SWEDEN | 29 YEARS OLD

3

Selma BACHA
LYON | FRANCE | 22 YEARS OLD

4

Sakina KARCHAOUI
PSG | FRANCE | 27 YEARS OLD

5

Ashley LAWRENCE
CHELSEA | CANADA | 28 YEARS OLD

1

Irene
PAREDES
BARCELONA | SPAIN | 32 YEARS OLD

CENTRE-BACKS
→ Cool, calm and composed
→ Big, powerful and strong
→ Tactically and technically excellent

2

Magdalena
ERIKSSON
BAYERN MUNICH | SWEDEN | 29 YEARS OLD

3

Wendie
RENARD
LYON | FRANCE | 33 YEARS OLD

4

Mapi
LEON
BARCELONA | SPAIN | 28 YEARS OLD

5
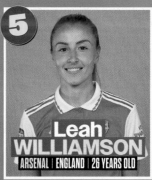
Leah
WILLIAMSON
ARSENAL | ENGLAND | 26 YEARS OLD

1

Alexia
PUTELLAS
BARCELONA | SPAIN | 29 YEARS OLD

MIDFIELDERS
→ Great balance, vision and close control
→ Confident, inventive and technically excellent
→ A creative and intelligent passer

2

Aitana
BONMATI
BARCELONA | SPAIN | 25 YEARS OLD

3

Lena
OBERDORF
WOLFSBURG | GERMANY | 21 YEARS OLD

4

Keira
WALSH
BARCELONA | ENGLAND | 26 YEARS OLD

5

Lina
MAGULL
BAYERN MUNICH | GERMANY | 29 YEARS OLD

1

Beth MEAD
ARSENAL | ENGLAND | 28 YEARS OLD

FORWARDS
→ Quick feet with a locker full of tricks
→ Amazing control, technique and vision
→ Creates goals, scores goals – a game-changer

2

Caroline Graham HANSEN
BARCELONA | NORWAY | 28 YEARS OLD

3

Catarina MACARIO
CHELSEA | USA | 23 YEARS OLD

4

Pernille HARDER
BAYERN MUNICH | DENMARK | 30 YEARS OLD

5

Alexandra POPP
WOLFSBURG | GERMANY | 32 YEARS OLD

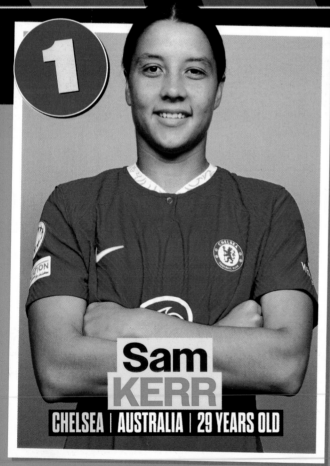

1

Sam KERR
CHELSEA | AUSTRALIA | 29 YEARS OLD

STRIKERS
→ Thunderous shot and sick technique
→ Clinical and ice-cool in front of goal
→ Outstanding movement and awareness

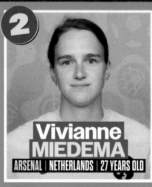

2

Vivianne MIEDEMA
ARSENAL | NETHERLANDS | 27 YEARS OLD

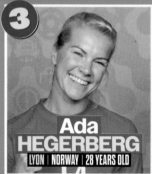

3

Ada HEGERBERG
LYON | NORWAY | 28 YEARS OLD

4

Marie-Antoinette KATOTO
PSG | FRANCE | 24 YEARS OLD

5

Asisat OSHOALA
BARCELONA | NIGERIA | 28 YEARS OLD

WHAT DO YOU THINK?

MY NO.1 KEEPER:

E.ARPS

MY NO.1 FULL-BACK:

BRONZE

MY NO.1 CENTRE-BACK:

WILLIAMSON

MY NO.1 MIDFIELDER:

PUTELLAS

MY NO.1 FORWARD:

MEAD

MY NO.1 STRIKER:

KERR

QUIZ ANSWERS!

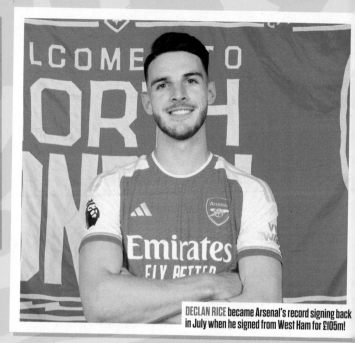

DECLAN RICE became Arsenal's record signing back in July when he signed from West Ham for £105m!

CHAMPIONS QUIZ!
From p9

1 B, 2 B, 3 C, 4 A, 5 B, 6 B, 7 B, 8 C, 9 B

MY SCORE [ ] OUT OF 9

SPOT THE BALL!
From p20

BALL 1

BALL 2

BALL 3

BALL 4

BALL ONE: **1C**, BALL TWO: **1F**
BALL THREE: **1B**, BALL FOUR: **1G**

MY SCORE [ ] OUT OF 4

STADIUM SEARCH!
From p21

S	T	A	N	F	O	R	D	B	R	I	D	G	E
R	U	H	N	T	I	P	H	F	E	R	W	S	X
L	O	V	T	G	Q	K	Z	V	T	R	E	D	A
J	O	F	C	L	V	A	P	J	B	O	C	T	E
N	R	X	M	O	L	I	N	E	U	X	R	C	C
Y	O	T	I	R	V	M	C	T	S	P	V	I	E
W	F	R	R	Y	I	T	F	I	D	X	I	T	L
K	F	L	A	N	E	X	E	N	C	Z	L	Y	T
B	A	I	T	D	S	H	K	R	I	U	L	G	I
O	R	U	G	E	D	C	Z	U	M	N	A	R	C
U	D	T	Y	S	O	F	H	K	L	B	P	C	P
M	O	L	D	A	N	F	I	E	L	D	A	U	A
S	L	D	G	F	D	U	D	Y	Y	R	N	R	R
G	O	O	D	I	S	O	N	P	A	R	K	D	K

MY SCORE [ ] OUT OF 12

GUESS WHO!
From p21

1 Carlo Ancelotti, 2 Pep Guardiola,
3 Erik ten Hag, 4 Mauricio Pochettino

MY SCORE [ ] OUT OF 4

BADGES & ANIMALS!
From p27

1 B, 2 C, 3 C, 4 A, 5 B, 6 C, 7 B, 8 B, 9 A

MY SCORE [ ] OUT OF 9

YEAR IN FOOTBALL!
From p39

1 C, 2 B, 3 A, 4 B, 5 B, 6 B, 7 B, 8 B, 9 C

MY SCORE [ ] OUT OF 9

BIG MONEY MEN!
From p47

1 B, 2 C, 3 B, 4 B, 5 A, 6 C, 7 A, 8 B, 9 B

MY SCORE [ ] OUT OF 9

QUIZ AN ADULT!
From p77-81

1: 1 A, 2 C, 3 B, 4 D

2: A David Batty, B Nick Barmby,
C Tim Flowers, D Dominic Matteo,
E Robbie Fowler

3 Howard Wilkinson

4: A Ipswich, B Sheffield Wednesday,
C Coventry

5 Man. City

6: A Chelsea, B Blackburn,
C Newcastle, D Man. United, E Coventry

7 Chelsea
8 Robert Lee
9 Juan Sebastian Veron
10 Clive Allen

ADULT HALF-TIME
SCORE [ ] OUT OF 23

11 B, 12 B, 13 C, 14 B, 15 D, 16 C, 17 C,
18 C, 19 D, 20 A

ADULT FULL-TIME
SCORE [ ] OUT OF 33

WHO THE HECK ARE YOU?
From p84

1 Martin Odegaard, 2 Harry Kane,
3 Mykhailo Mudryk, 4 Jarrod Bowen,
5 Erling Haaland, 6 Jordan Pickford,
7 Alessia Russo, 8 Antony,
9 Bruno Guimaraes

MY SCORE [ ] OUT OF 9

MATCH OF THE DAY MAGAZINE

Telephone 020 7150 5513
Email inbox@motdmag.com

Editor — Mark Parry
Deputy editor — Jake Wilson
Senior art editor — Blue Buxton
Senior designer — Bradley Wooldridge
Annual designer — Pete Rogers
Features editor — Sarah Johnson

Editorial assistant — Poppy Treadaway
Production editors — James Bandy, Will Demetriou

Publishing Director — Alex Coates-Newman
Assistant Publisher — Igrain Roberts
Annual images — Getty Images

BBC Books an imprint of Ebury Publishing 20 Vauxhall Bridge Road London SW1V 2SA. BBC Books is part of the Penguin Random House group of companies whose addresses can be found at global.penguinrandomhouse.com. Copyright © Match Of The Day magazine 2023. First published by BBC Books in 2023 www.penguin.co.uk. A CIP catalogue record for this book is available from the British Library. ISBN 9781785948374. Commissioning editor: Albert DePetrillo; project editor: Stadman Banerjee; production: Phil Spencer. Printed and bound in Italy by Elcograf S.p.A. The authorised representative in the EEA is Penguin Random House Ireland, Morrison Chambers, 32 Nassau Street, Dublin D02 YH68. Penguin Random House is committed to a sustainable future for our business our readers and our planet. This book is made from Forest Stewardship Council ® certified paper.

BBC

BBC Match of the Day Magazine is published by Immediate Media Company London Limited under licence from BBC Studios Distribution Limited. © Immediate Media Company London Limited 2023.

ERLING HAALAND

NORWAY

MATCH OF THE DAY MAGAZINE

WORLD DREAM TEAM!

STRIKER

MY PREDICTIONS FOR 2023-24!

We want you to make the big calls about what's going to happen this season!

MY FACT FILE!

NAME: Freddie

AGE: 10 **HOME TOWN:** Cullen

FAVOURITE TEAM: England

FAVOURITE PLAYER: Messi

STICK A PHOTO OF YOURSELF HERE

1 WHO WILL WIN THE PREMIER LEAGUE?

Villa

Man. City have won the Prem three years in a row, and in five of the last six seasons. Can anyone stop them?

2022-23 WINNER: MAN. CITY

2 WHO WILL WIN THE GOLDEN BOOT?

HAALAND

Erling Haaland's 36 goals last term were the most scored by anyone since the Premier League began in 1992!

2022-23 WINNER: ERLING HAALAND, MAN. CITY

3 WHO WILL BE PREMIER LEAGUE PLAYER OF THE YEAR?

Watkins

This is the award voted for by all Premier League players — it's the players' very own hero of the season!

2022-23 WINNER: ERLING HAALAND, MAN. CITY

4 WHO WILL WIN THE FA CUP?

The FA Cup was part two of Man. City's treble when they beat city rivals United in June 2023. A total of 44 different clubs have won the cup — but who will it be in 2024?

2022-23 WINNER: MAN. CITY

5 WHO WILL WIN THE EFL CUP?

?

This has been won by one of the Manchester clubs in seven of the last eight seasons, with City claiming five wins and United two. Who'll be celebrating this season?

2022-23 WINNER: MAN. UNITED